SINCERELY, ROOM 111

Voices of a New Era

AMERICAN LITERATURE
STUDENTS OF ROOM 111
AT HANFORD HIGH SCHOOL,
RICHLAND, WA

outskirts
press

For those teens whose voices are not heard

and

for those still searching for their voice

Foreword

On March 16th, 2020, over a million students in Washington State walked into their school building, not realizing that would be the last time they would set foot in a school for almost a year. It would be the last time they would eat school lunch with their friends, study frantically in the library before a major quiz, skip class, play a pickup game of basketball at lunch, take part in a seminar, hold the hand of their girlfriend, or walk into a classroom tardy.

On March 17, 2020, the students and their peers would have their lives turned upside down when Governor Inslee made the decision to close all schools to slow the spread of the coronavirus.

These students were officially living in a pandemic – something none of us had ever experienced. These students were asked to do something that we as adults had never navigated. They were asked to take on the challenge of learning fully remotely and online. We asked them to learn new technology, attend, stay engaged, achieve passing grades, while hopefully dodging the impacts of the virus itself. These students lost loved ones, saw their families struggle financially, had school and community activities and sports ripped from their lives, and saw their social lives drastically impacted.

As a veteran educator, I knew this shutdown would have a significantly negative impact on students academically, financially, socially, and emotionally. We will only discover the true impact down the road when we see the data. We are still trying to find what the new "normal" looks like for students and education.

When Phil Cioppa approached me about putting together this book capturing students' experiences during this pandemic, I was eager to jump in and see what they could do. To say I have been impressed is an understatement. These students were able to put their fears, sadness, concerns, and regrets on paper, in stories, poems, and artwork. This all comes down to trust – and these students trusted Phil to take them on this journey. They trusted him enough to showcase their vulnerability, and they trusted him enough to put their hearts on the page. They trusted him enough to take what has probably been one of the worst things to happen in their lives and use their voices to let other teenagers know they are not alone.

I truly appreciate the heart that Phil Cioppa possesses for his students and their craft. Phil is creating lifelong bonds and memories for these students, and the impact will be felt for years to come. Dive in with us as we take a look into the thoughts and feelings of these teenagers. Their words, wisdom, thoughtfulness, and intentionality are reflected in every word. I hope you all enjoy reading them as much as I have. Enjoy!

Tiffany Spencer
Vice Principal
Hanford High School

Introduction

The COVID-19 pandemic has left many numb. Teens have borne the great brunt of this given the past two years. Although endurance has been a challenge, out of this pandemic has risen an abundant amount of goodness. It is from that goodness that the conception and compilation of this book came to fruition.

I asked my students to reflect upon the suffering and difficulties that teens have, and are facing during this present pandemic, and to develop what they felt was the best piece of advice that they could offer other teens. I was amazed at their poignancy and wisdom. We spoke about how we could share this information, and after some investigation, we decided to publish their thoughts and feelings.

At times, we as parents and teachers forget that we can learn from teens just as they learn from us. While they take the best of what we model and use that to grow into ethical and good citizens, they also come to realize that they have a voice. When teens wish to help other teens, it is evident that we, as a community, are doing something right.

This book was far from a singular effort, nor was it just the effort of the 100+ students who participated in this project. On behalf of the students involved in this project, I want to express my deep appreciation to the Richland School District's administrative team who have encouraged this project to go forward. I want to thank Mr. Tory Christensen, Principal of Hanford High School, for his generosity and support. I also want to thank Ms. Chelsea Evans, my colleague in the English Language Arts Department, for her invaluable assistance with making sure the sketches and photograph in this book were ready for the publisher. In a special way I want to thank my supervisor, Ms. Tiffany Spencer, Vice Principal, for her encouragement, energy, and tremendous support she has offered this project. Finally, I want to thank one of our parents, Mr. Tom Rickey, who edited this book with me and gave a great deal of his time to work on this project. Tom's kindness and generosity are immeasurable!

I came to Hanford High School this year (2021-22) as an English Language Arts teacher and have been privileged to teach American Literature to 11th grade students. They are European-American, African-American, Mexican-American, Latin-American, Native-American, and Asian-American. They represent the wonderful tapestry of our community. I have taught thousands of incredible students, and I count this group of young people among them.

As the students will tell you, I consider them "my kids." As is the culture of Richland School District, we only want the best for our students, so it was very easy to begin to teach here. Since they are "my kids," my interest in them extends far beyond my classroom, any other class, and even our school. They are each unique and special. They have enriched my life greatly, and I believe you will find that their honesty and candor enrich yours as well. They have something to say, and we are called to listen to them. They are not only our future, but they are our "now"! Above all else, let's make sure we always let young people know that they are loved!

Phil Cioppa
English Language Arts
Hanford High School
Richland, WA

Abigail

Find something to look forward to. I spent 2–5 hours after online class meetings just doing homework to keep myself from falling behind. Every time I logged off I wanted to throw my computer into the garbage can and crawl back into my warm bed, but life doesn't work that way. If you want to reach your goals, you have to do the work. Having a goal in mind gives you that motivation to get stuff done. I would always tell myself that "If I want to reach my goals and get my dream career, I have to do all the work to get there... starting with this stupid homework assignment." So I did it; I did all of them. Though it took a major toll on my mental health, I did it all. By keeping my goals in mind, I continue to succeed and try as hard as I can. Even though these past few years have been so full of garbage, I would like it if you tried to set a goal for yourself, whether it's making your bed in the morning, a career goal, or to become healthier – choose something to help you know that you can power through. I know you can.

Adam

Advice I will offer to you in current times is to think for yourself. Do not get swept into the crowd, do not let it decide your opinions, and most importantly, do not let it decide your view of right and wrong. You see, the crowd is like chess pieces being used by evil players. They will promote things within this crowd to destroy those who are a part of it. You may be thinking to yourself, "What are you talking about?" To that I will ask you how you have felt emotionally and physically. What are the people around you like? Do they seem happy, healthy? I would assume the answer is no, and this is because of those evil players that have gripped the game of life. This is not how things used to be. People used to have families, they had community. The ironic thing is, the things that are good for us are seen as bad. This is by design. Now that I have told you that it is good for you to defy social norms, there is one more thing you can do. You see, it is likely not enough to simply defy the group. Your community/families could very well be a part of it. You must do what you can to stop this society from being driven by lies and evil. There will be times where you think maybe you shouldn't do anything, perhaps ignore it, but you must know that these thoughts are just another one of their weapons, just another way for them to numb you as they destroy you and the ones around you. As this book ages through time, I imagine the meaning of these words I write today will be more apparent.

Aiden

You and me both, man – don't worry, I suffer the same as you, maybe less or in a greater way. But I feel that stress and struggle with school because it's just so overwhelming and they expect so much from us and we don't have that time for school, sports, and friends. Just so much goes on in our little lives and then you have to worry about family issues sometimes. I totally get it. I drive 30 minutes to school everyday while taking my sister to school everyday so make that a 45-minute drive. Now that's an hour and a half out of my day just for a drive. Add 1 to 3 hours of school work and I just can't stand it. It drives me nuts so don't think you're alone.

And to all others who suffer with grades, I am there too. They expect so much for things that we most likely will never use again and then grade us based on if we memorized it over a span of 3 weeks. Then we have to memorize it after 4 and a half months and have to memorize it all during a school year to take a test that we require for college and need a high score to even get into a good college. But who knows, maybe we can grow up and do a job where we don't do the same exact thing over and over again every single day and hope we don't go insane. I know life can be stressful but you and I both need to come together and compose our breaths and worry about today and prepare for tomorrow. Together we can all do it and thrive for ourselves and our families, creating a better environment for our kids to grow up in.

Alex Ly

Life is beautiful, confusing, and terrifying. We can never tell if things are starting to look bright, or if the world is crumbling before our eyes. That being said, I believe our generation is the first with the potential to fix the problems that plague our modern world. Some of these obstacles have been natural, others have been burdened onto us by those who came before, and some we have burdened onto ourselves. In the end, we will prevail because quitting isn't an option. When you confront an obstacle in your own life, you don't push through it to look strong or inspirational, you push through it because you have no other choice. We must do the same if we plan on healing this broken world.

Alex L.

Suppose you and I and all the other teens in the world were not financially sound. I would tell you that it's essential to learn and start now. Because if you don't start now, it may be hard when you become an adult and get that first house or home or even maybe that first car.

See, most teens lack money, but there are many ways to earn money. Working is one way, or maybe getting a commission where you're paid by how well the work is done. There are a couple of great ways for me, you, or any teen to earn money and not struggle with cash or finances.

Amanda

The advice that I want teens to have is that people treat you how they feel about you. During the pandemic, you probably lost a number of your friends. Most of us did. Now, coming out of the pandemic, we are finding our new circle and finding new people to associate ourselves with. My advice to you in this time of recovery and discovery is: do not associate yourself with people who bring more bad than good into your life.

When people show you that they do not value you, do not keep choosing to keep them in your life. People treat you how they feel about you, so don't make excuses for their negative behavior and actions, and be cautious about which of their excuses you believe. The people you are meant to keep in your life will treat you with value and make you feel better, not worse.

Anabelle

The Covid-19 pandemic has taken a toll on all of us; you're not alone. People underestimate your feelings as a teen simply because you are young. Understanding your brain as a teen is essential for your upcoming actions and social life. Every teen thinks their brain is fully developed when it actually isn't. I learned in psychology that your brain doesn't fully develop until age 25. Psychology has taught me a lot about my brain and others. I have been taught that the teen and adult brain are dramatically different to the point where they use different parts of the brain. Teens use their amygdala while adults use their prefrontal cortex. In simpler terms, we use our emotions to think while adults use their decision-making center.

We need to start at home before jumping into the big social world. If you know how to socialize with your parents, you most likely know how to associate with other people. To thrive during this pandemic or even after, we need to want that growth in our lives. Understanding your brain is good, but understanding your feelings will boost you to find what you need to fix or grow. Most people will be hard to talk to, and you will have to limit the people you talk to, but that does not mean no one is there for you.

They just don't know how to help you. Consider what I say: not everyone has to suffer during or after Covid. Make it an opportunity for you to strive and learn from it.

Bradley

BRADLEY

Anthony

Obstacles: Life is full of them and I hate them. There is only one thing I hate more than obstacles and that is gas prices – but even that is an obstacle, and obstacles are meant to be overcome. Throughout my life, I have faced many obstacles, some bigger than others, but that's just life. You've never heard anybody say life was fair or easy because it's not. Even though nobody likes obstacles, without them life would be boring and gray. Just think – without controversy, everything would be handed to you without having to work for it and that's not fun. Life is like a game and the levels get harder as you get older; without challenges (obstacles) the game gets boring and not fun anymore.

Now there is a bad side to obstacles that can chew you up and spit you right back out with ease. You may feel like you got dealt a bad hand in life, but just know that whatever you are going through, there is someone out there going through a lot worse. We all have different obstacles in life. Some of them might beat you up so badly that you want to give up, but you have to keep fighting and not let it get the best of you. Any mountain can be climbed, any river can be crossed, and every obstacle can be overcome – it just comes down to how hard you try.

Ava P.

The most important advice that I could offer to teenagers is to focus on building strong and reliable connections with your friends and family. By doing this you can have the assurance that when you make those tough and impactful life decisions, that you will be fully supported no matter what happens. These types of connections can give teenagers the confidence going onto the next chapter of their lives knowing that no matter where they end up, they will always have those connections to guide and support them. Teens overall have a lot of anxiety worrying about making the wrong decision about their future. Having strong relation-ships with their peers and relatives might ease some of those worries by letting teens know they won't be judged. Good friendships can last a lifetime – through the highs and lows – but with the right people it can be a lot more bearable.

Ava W.

As your childhood becomes a more distant memory, the most important thing you can do to prepare yourself for the rest of your life is to get to know yourself. Having a good sense of self will help you in all aspects of your life. It will help you to overcome obstacles when you know what keeps you going. Keeping tabs on yourself will help in the constant battle to maintain your mental health. To know how to care for yourself, what triggers you, and what can pull you out of a dark place. Knowing what interests you, and what brings you joy, will help you as you turn 18 and everyone around you tells you to figure out what to do with the rest of your life – and it will help as you continue to age and are still trying to figure that out.

Aydan

Take care of yourself because you matter. I say this because many people make themselves feel worthless or less than they are. The reality is when people put themselves down, that is the beginning of the path of constant decline. This path of decline is easy to start but hard to end. Many get stuck with the twists and turns and find themselves lost in what they can only see as worthlessness. Teens often find themselves in this situation in their lives where they can't even find meaning. Teens in the pandemic are starting to struggle with this more often. To prevent walking on this path, teens need to value themselves more. First, teens must understand nothing is perfect in this world. Second, instead of focusing on the negatives, they should focus on the positive. Third, teens must know life is a long journey full of obstacles. After each obstacle, teens are a step closer to their own goals. They must keep pushing forward because, in the end, all the hard work pays off.

Briella

The world is so full of fear, judgment, and anger. My advice to you is honestly, try to focus on the positives in your life. Trust me I know that is easier said than it is done but it really can be a game changer in a lot of ways. Not only focusing on the positive things in your life but it is really important to focus on being who you want to be and improving yourself. Whatever that may mean to you, just do what you feel is right and do the best you can. More importantly, self improvement can really positively change your whole teenage experience. I know sometimes it can feel like there is nothing you can do to improve your life but that's just it, you can do everything to change who you are to be the person you want to be. You really are the only one who can change the things that need to be changed in order to love yourself. No one else can do that for you, especially if they don't know what you need in order to be happy and succeed. Things will get better and your life will begin to look up, but first you have to acknowledge the pain and suffering. You need to do this to be able to change and to do the things you need to do to be content with your life.

Brooklyn

My advice for other teens trying to overcome obstacles is to have a strong support system and have people you know you can go to when you need to talk or get away for a while. The second is to never give up! We all go through trials in our lives, and we can either learn and grow from them, or they can break us down and defeat us. The third is to have faith in yourself and your strength; you are stronger and smarter than you realize. It may be hard now, but a year from now, it will be better! The final thing is to look forward to the future. Don't dwell in the past; your future is bright. What happened yesterday or last week does not determine what you do today or tomorrow; you make your own choices; you determine your future! So make good choices and cherish today's gift no matter how hard it is; remember you are loved, and you have a purpose!

Bryan

If I was talking to my teen self about overcoming obstacles, my main thing would be to just make sure that if you are struggling with anything, to make sure you talk to adults. Adults will help you get through anything you're struggling with, like mental health. Another thing is just breathing and relaxing, just thinking of all the good things in the world – that helps a lot. You can also go and talk to your friends, because they are the same age as you, and live almost the same life and some know what you are going through. The last thing I can say is whatever your favorite hobbies or favorite sports are, just play those to get your mind off what you're going through.

Caden C.

We've all had a dream before, whether it was to fight fires, lead a nation, help kids with a terminal disease, or any other imaginable idea. Our dreams are very fickle things: One day it's to study the depths of the ocean, the next it's to care for animals and nurse them back to health. Sometimes it's to explore the stars, as it had been with me. What you have to realize is that they are a reflection of how you view yourself, and how you will view yourself in the future.

Your dreams are the modeling clay of civilization and most people don't even realize it. Yet too many fall into the same trap. All too often has someone fallen short of their dreams because they didn't take the risks, many times because they didn't want to be uncomfortable or couldn't afford to put themselves in a precarious situation. Now, under no circumstances am I saying that our dreams are unachievable; someone with enough motivation to try is someone who will succeed. Hopefully, that someone is you.

Caden N.

It is saddening to go throughout school and hear students say the phrase, "I hate my life." Though most teens don't really mean it, teens today need to understand that life is to be cherished and loved. Life can be difficult and disheartening at times, but there will always be times when it's great to be alive. Don't let the hard times drag you down and make you miserable. Your life is your own and you can make it to be the best life you can. If you are dissatisfied with your life, then go out and make it a life you can love, because your life is only the way you make it to be. It may be hard to change but in the end it will make you happier. Love your life and make it one that makes you happy.

Caleb

Knowing how to differentiate between truth and opinion is very essential in today's world. With so many "facts" being shared about so many controversial topics, it gets difficult to find the actual truth and discover what I really believe. We need more people who decide to purely share the truth. In the end, the truth is all that matters. You need to make the effort to find and share the truth. With so much contention in today's world, opinions, bias, and pride only get in the way of solving our problems. You can be the problem solver if you simply live by the facts. You and I must be truly informed to make the difference that can be made.

Calvin

I feel that a good friend can change a person. It can change how they see the world, others, and themselves. A friend can change your perspective and personality just by being there for you and helping you. There are all types of friends that you can have. The one that will impact you the most is the one that will be there for you any time. A great friend will follow this quote. "All of the people around me hug me when I win, but my friend. All of the people around me ignore me, but my friend hugs me." To me, that is a good friend, someone that will be there for you no matter what.

I have many friends, but only 2 of them know when I am truly sad. They will react by trying their best to make me feel good. When you look at your friends, look for the people who have been with you the most and never left you. That is a true friend, and don't lose them because they will be with you forever.

Carolynn

How to overcome some obstacles of Covid-19? One way is keeping yourself busy but in a good way. You don't want to become so busy that you feel stressed or overwhelmed, but you could find a hobby or something that you enjoy doing. Some things that helped me get through these tough times are keeping in touch with friends. I am always with my family so knowing that I can communicate with my friends through social media was very helpful. Another thing that was very fun to pass time was online shopping.

Casey

I think the most important thing for a teen to know is to make better friends, not more friends. I have some amazing friends I've had since elementary school, and even some before that, who have stuck with me through everything. Having someone you can always go and talk to who is closer in age with you can be way easier than trying to go and talk to an adult. People might think it's "cool" to have tons of friends but unless they are all honest great friends, then it doesn't matter. After you leave high school, lots of people won't talk to anyone they went to school with, but if you have people who you are super close with, you will probably still talk to them.

Chloe

Older generations, movies, and other media often refer to the teenage years of one's life as "the golden days" or their "prime." This makes you feel terrible, that you've lost these precious years to Covid. You think this is supposed to be the happiest time in your life, so why have you never felt worse? This thinking puts you in the mindset that it only gets worse from here. When you are already so incredibly low, the thought of getting worse is detrimental to you. However, in all honesty you decide if it gets worse. Obviously there are tragedies that are out of your control but you do have the choice to keep going, and as you keep going the chances that something good is going to come your way get greater and greater. If you spend all your time in your head about minor things and stressing over everything that crosses your path, are you ever going to be able to fully enjoy anything? Make your life how you want your life to be. Being a teenager should not be full of stress, it should be full of excitement and fun and rebellion. Enjoy living in the moment and making mistakes while you're still young enough to fix them. Life lessons are learned through living your own life, not other people telling you how.

Cole

My piece of advice for teens would be to stay close with family and friends. Being alone during times like Covid makes it hard on you if you don't socialize. Staying in touch with people is key to making it because of all the drama and politics that goes on in pandemics. Having your friends and family there makes it so you don't have to think about those things as much as you would without them. Just remember, you're not alone. There's always someone there for you.

Corbett

When I turned 16, I got a debit card with $1600 of my hard-earned money on it. I loved the idea of a debit card because it gave me freedom. I could buy whatever I wanted from wherever I wanted. A debit card gave me lots of opportunities to purchase to my heart's content, but I promised myself I would save my money. Well, I tried to keep my promise to save money, but in the end the urge to spend and buy new things tempted me into spending all my money on stuff I didn't really need.

Losing all of my money taught me to be better with my money. Now that I am getting closer to adulthood, I realize that saving money, spending wisely, and earning money is boring and not very fun but you've got to do it. You don't have to make life all about money. You also don't need to be an all-out cheapskate to make your way through life. Just don't do what I did and spend over a thousand dollars on stuff you don't need.

Crystal

Times have been tough with the pandemic. Life has been turned and twisted in a million ways. Because of this I have a piece of advice for you to help get through this insanity as well as helping with the rest of your life. Find something that makes you happy. It doesn't have to be productive, and it doesn't have to be something serious. Simply find something that you can do that makes you happy and doesn't feel like a chore.

Play a video game or two that makes you happy to play. Watch a show that makes you laugh, read comics, read books or even fan fiction. If you want, it can even change or be a multitude of activities. Just find something that you can look forward to and motivates you to get through even your most difficult of days. Life can be rough and you may question if it's worth living sometimes, but having that one thing that pushes your troubles away temporarily and can bring you happiness in minutes is crucial to getting through those troubling times until you reach brighter days. Having something that makes you happy, that you can always look forward to, will be your stable lighthouse for even the roughest of storms that exist in the torrents of your mind.

Damian

During Covid, I felt isolated and alone for a while. I was not seeing any of my friends, just sitting around days blending into the next. I do drama. I am a national thespian of Troupe 3183, and I miss being on the stage and working with my friends, so I wanted to find a new outlet. So I bought a ring light and a new phone to record myself and post it on my youtube. I was and still am proud of my first video. It went very well, and my friends loved it and thought it was hilarious, so I started to make all the videos I could. I enjoyed making them. It made me happy for the first time in the pandemic. Then I made an acting account on Instagram where I could just post anything I wanted that was acting, and it is still so fun just to turn on my camera and just go. I wish people would try to perform. Many of you do though you don't realize it, and it hurts me when you are in a fixed mindset or that you don't want to because you'll be embarrassed. I think it's essential to not care about what others think of you because it's obscured. You can do anything you want if you put in the work and effort. YOU can do whatever you want.

David

Keep close friends, not more friends
In a pandemic where we see everything through a new lens
We try to restore relationships with those
we love to make amends
And say goodbye to those we lost while Covid spreads
We go through life just wanting to be in our beds
Everything we see and hear on TV just gets in our heads
We have to be careful of everything we say
to make no offends
That's why we must keep our close friends

Our friends help lift us up when we're down
They give us worth like a crown
They help us not to frown, no matter how down
They make us laugh like a clown
When no one responds like a ghost town
Our friends will be down, to come to town
To laugh
To love
To care

Dawson

If you want to improve your life, figure out what things you have control over and try to fix them. In a speech by Jordan Peterson, he said to "Start small. Ask yourself a few questions: Have you taken full advantage of the opportunities offered to you? Are you working to your fullest capacity at school or at work? Have you, in other words, set your own house in order? If the answer is no, try this: stop doing what you know to be wrong. Stop today. Don't waste time asking how you know that what you're doing is wrong. Inopportune questioning can confuse without enlightening, and deflect you from action. You can know something is right or wrong without knowing why."*

In the same speech, Peterson says that "In my three decades as a professor and clinical psychologist, I have learned that there are two fundamental attitudes toward life and its sorrows. Those with the first attitude blame the world. Those with the second ask what they could do differently."* Start today and spend a few minutes writing a simple list of problems you can fix.

Seeing everything on a list will give you more clarity and help you focus on the issues you want to fix. Fixing the problems will make you a more mature person and will allow you to pursue more challenging areas of your life.

*https://assets.ctfassets.net/qnesrjodfi80/TuhZfb9 6aQg2GwWu2I0SQ/2145f63927d07515b51dab66 7f782492/peterson-fix_yourself-transcript.pdf (https:// youtu.be/o73pqQ9Gzt4)

Easton

During this pandemic and the hard times we are all going through, I think we can all agree we have advice we would like to give to help people get through this. I would have to say that pushing through school and all the work that we are going to get can be very hard. We all know that kids are overwhelmed with the school-work we now have, and not getting a complete year last year really put a delay in our learning path for high school. My advice would be to just look at it day by day, do what you can to make it through today and always try your hardest. Even when times get tough and you may not get the scores you want, keep pushing and do what you can.

Elizabeth

As a teenager, this time of life is full of questions and doubts about sexual orientation. Expectations to be straight or to even be interested in the idea of romantic or sexual relationships are ever-present and make it increasingly difficult to figure out where you fall. The best thing one can do when questioning their sexuality is researching the meanings behind the labels in the LGBTQ+ community. If you can, talk to someone you trust who has experienced the same problems with sexual orientation in the past. Learning about the definitions of labels like bisexual, demisexual, gay, lesbian, asexual, etc., can help one form what they are attracted to or not into words. Finding a comfortable label can be the first step in further discovering yourself. If you find later on in your life that a label doesn't quite fit, you can always switch to one that works better. Finding out what you identify as can then bring you to others who identify similarly and have cleared doubt about their own orientation. There will always be someone who once had the same questions about their sexual orientation, and asking for their advice on how they found themselves can help immensely. Above all, remember that no matter what you think you might be sexually, you're not alone in your situation.

Emily

Who are you? Who am I? Whatever you want to do or be in life... do it, live it. With all the obstacles we overcome as teenagers, we deserve to live a little. But to be able to live, we need to stay who we are and never change for anyone. Changing to someone you aren't is unhealthy and can cause you stress and anxiety about what someone else thinks of you, which doesn't allow you to be the person you were born to be. Staying "you" is one of the most important parts of being a teenager, this is when you get to find the "true you." When you go to school, work, or whatever and you see that one person that you would want to be exactly like, don't think like that. You don't want to be them — you want to be you. You don't know their life and you don't need to, the only opinion that matters is yours.

Emma

The most important thing I learned during the Covid-19 pandemic is how important social interaction and being with your friends are. When you are isolated for so long you begin to realize how important social interaction is, even if it is going to the grocery store. This made a huge impact on teens by having more mental health problems. Even though we all hate to admit it, we genuinely missed going to school and the interactions we had with people. Not seeing any one and being stuck with your family for so long honestly drives you insane. From my personal experience, losing your friends is one of the greatest pains I have ever felt. So my greatest advice is to keep your friends close because holding on to your friends will do you great justice in the future.

Gaige

If I were to share a piece of advice to someone in the same situation I was in, I would say "It's OK to be vulnerable." Don't be afraid to be open and honest with not only others but with yourself. It's typical for people our age to feel like all these new responsibilities as young adults are all up to us but they're not. It's impossible to go about living in this day and age without feeling overwhelmed, stressed, and hopeless. All these feelings are natural but don't let them linger. Trust in the people you care about to help guide you through times of uncertainty.

Gannon

It is human nature to compare ourselves to others, especially teens. It is true comparing ourselves to others is a factor of finding your own identity but only to an extent. When teens see other teens living the life they want, it can be detrimental to themselves. They see teens their age with materialistic things they can't have and start to question themselves. It can seem as if they are fading into a false reality. Aristotle once said, "Man is by nature a social animal; an individual who is unsocial naturally and not accidentally is either beneath our notice or more than human. Society is something that precedes the individual."

Garrett

As a teenager the best way to overcome any obstacle is staying positive. There is no way you're going to get over it if you're being dismissive and gloomy 24/7. Most obstacles you usually face are in school and having to do massive amounts of homework from different classes even though we just had a full day of school. Every teen goes through this type of thing most of the time. You just have to be optimistic about things and have a good outlook instead of being down on yourself.

Gianna

the wind flitters sharply between my numb fingers

a reminder that i am still here

alive and breathing

but i feel so tired

wisps of my hair whip against my face

and i wonder to myself

if there's really any point anymore

if this constant cold and darkness is worth it

but then there's a tingling warmth

burning up through my hands and to my face

like a dancing wildfire on my skin

and i look up and see the sun

peeking through the clouds

on this life-barren, somber day

the sun still came to say hello

as if it's telling me that it's still here too

and i still feel so tired

but it's okay

because i have the sun

and its sanguine arms of light embracing me

Gianni B.

You are experiencing a time that your grandkids will read about in history books. What keeps me motivated during this time is remembering no matter how bad you think your situation is, there is always somebody that has it worse. I am grateful that my biggest problem is Covid, when there are people that wake up not knowing where they're going to sleep that night or when the next time they will have a hot meal. You might be feeling like nothing will ever get better but trust me, it does. In the end something bad can always lead to something good that can change your life for the better.

Gianni F.

I believe the most important advice I could give to teenagers right now is to make good friends now, to find a group that you feel comfortable around and trust. These friends will be your most important asset in life, they will always be there and always help you when you're in need because they love you and want to see you succeed. They will be there for you during tough times to help you through them, provide solutions, and be a shoulder to cry on if you need it. Having good friends also helps to stop feelings of depression and anxiety, which seem to be more and more common nowadays. Many people will say that friends are hard to make the later in life you try, so it's even more important to make those good friends now. Even with all the serious reasons to make good friends, an important one is just to have people you can have fun with.

Grace

Quarantine

Days turn to weeks

Turn to months

Turn to years

To be alone for so long I wish not on anyone

Fleeting time, Life gone

The Mind spiraling and twisting

Whispering thoughts and temptations no one will know

Each day becoming a repetitive cycle

Cut off from reality and society

Like an old foggy memory

Loneliness becoming a constant lingering presence

The yearning to feel what we once took for granted

Dark circles under the tired eyes of students

Due to the long hours spent staring into a screen

Hoping for a future

That will always be uncertain

Life has not gone according to plan

And it never will

But that's okay

Because after every fire

Means new Growth, Flourishment, and Love

Hannah

The best advice I can give you is to take care of your health. In the beginning of the Covid-19 pandemic I was tired of feeling physically sick and exhausted so I decided to change my habits. For the first time I made my health a priority and started eating healthier and exercising. I almost immediately enjoyed the benefits both physically and mentally. The choice to change my habits to prioritize my health changed my life.

Prioritizing your health will give you the confidence and ability to change your life for the better. With poor health becoming a tremendous problem in the United States, taking care of your health can help protect you from the increasing number of physical and mental diseases. Changing your habits in your teenage years will not only help you now in life, but will prepare you for a healthy lifestyle in adulthood. Although changing what is familiar to us is hard, I can promise you that the struggle is worth it. I know as you take steps towards a healthier lifestyle, not only will you be happier but you will be able to change your life.

Hayden

How to overcome obstacles: An example is that teens need to learn to say NO to peer pressure. You need to stand up and learn to say NO because one day some kid will walk up to you and say that you should do this thing, and you know that you will get in trouble from this, but you never learned how to say NO because you're scared of not fitting in with teens your age.

I had this one friend who invited me to a party which I knew would have some sort of drugs. I just said that I already had plans and I didn't really talk to him after that because I knew that later on, I would get in trouble because of him. So now I know to choose your friends wisely and say no when you know it's bad. You can always figure a way around. Say that you are busy that day or you're grounded or say that your mom doesn't want you out that day. There are always ways to NO without saying NO.

Heather

Take things one step at a time. It is hard to manage homework along with work, school, extracurricular activities, and relationships in your lives. Try to focus on one thing at a time; it is a lot easier to manage if you aren't looking at everything at once. Also, having a list with what you prioritize the most, then using that as your guide can be really helpful. Some things may have to be sacrificed but you will be able to fit in what is most important to you. If you are determined, focused, and stay calm, you will be able to find a balance that works for you. It is hard now but it will calm down, you just have to stay strong.

Hussain

In terms of advice I can give to you all, I'm not sure I'm very qualified. I don't have much experience with anything. The coronavirus made me lose an entire year that I wish I could have gotten back. However, I can tell you all one thing. Don't make enemies. I suppose you could substitute this with "Don't burn any bridges." Generally, it is the same idea. The same way you don't want to burn a bridge after crossing it (which usually would not work since most bridges are made of stone), you do not want to make any enemies.

One way to think of this is, more enemies makes more inconvenience. You already have to deal with grades, extracurriculars, maybe a job, chores, and maintaining friendships. One more person who wants to drive you to failure is just annoying. I am speaking from experience, and it is way easier to not hate people. The thing about bridges, too, is that burnt bridges cannot actively go out to harm you. Frankly, you don't have to follow this advice, but I personally think it would be a good idea.

Hutton

Something that I would tell a teen who is struggling through the Covid-19 pandemic is to just stop worrying about small things that really shouldn't matter and just keep going no matter what. Many people worry so much about what others think of them that it stops them from doing what they want to do. I just think people should do what they want and not worry about what others think of them, because no matter what you do in life, people will judge you for it, so why worry about it? People just need to just keep going on no matter what. Even if you're going through the worst time of your life and feel like you are never going to get better, eventually things will change and you will feel better. Having a hobby that can help you keep your mind off things and can help you get through those hard times – even if it doesn't feel like it is helping, it is.

Jack

Your character and personality are a part of you and they reflect how you see the world. You may not realize it, but the way you act every day is influenced greatly by how you perceive the environment with which you interact. Your eyes may stay the same, but your opinions act as lenses that drastically change how you see everything. Those lenses may be completely original, developed entirely by yourself, but they are always under stress from the social environments we are present in. Any entity, no matter how predominant or insignificant, can and will modify how you see the world. Even though constant external influence is inevitable, you are not being coerced into following the dominant opinion and at any point you can re-evaluate your values and perception. I believe that the most important element of living in our society is to be able to recognize when our opinions are not our own. When we live with borrowed opinions, we are unable to live truly as ourselves. Despite the vast amount of external pressure and influence you may experience, every single person can choose how they want to live and no one else can be the judge of that.

Jacob

Don't let people's opinions change who you are. When I was younger I used to think people's opinions about me mattered. Maybe it would make me cooler, maybe I would fit in more. I'm going to say this: What people think about you doesn't matter, it doesn't make you cooler, it won't help you fit in. All I want to tell you guys is be yourself; don't change for anyone, Fitting in is dumb, and being cool won't make you feel any different. I've had the feeling of not fitting in; it made me feel like an outcast. It's the feeling of being left out; nobody invites you anywhere and nobody wants to hang out with you. It's never a good feeling but as you grow up your style changes. My dad told me that and he has helped me through the years. And if you still feel like an outcast, there will be people who like the same things as you. I felt like an outcast until I was six years old, then I found a group of friends that I'm still friends with to this day.

Jase

I don't have much to give in advice to many big problems teens face. But I do know one thing and that is sleep. Through most of my teen years at school, I haven't gotten any sleep. This is mostly because of my choices, and let me tell you, it's not fun. Having no energy for anything and feeling like you're going to pass out at any second does not feel good. As I write this, my ability to think properly is being impaired. So here's my advice to you if you want to be able to work properly and focus: Get over eight hours of sleep or end up feeling what I feel.

Joel

Should teens care what other people think? I think teens should not care about what others think because teens should live the way they want to live without anyone caring. Teens should not care because they could get insecure about themselves. It could also affect their attitude by bringing them down. Lastly, it could make them change their goals. Teens already have to worry about not getting through the pandemic. Teens should not be caring about what others think about them.

Joey K.

What I didn't know, what advice I needed a long time ago, was to learn when to walk away and not look back. I and many others will force ourselves into situations that are unbeneficial to ourselves mentally, physically, or even financially. We keep ourselves in these situations because we may fear the backlash, the consequences, the repercussions, the backlash, or even the loss. We tell ourselves the silent suffering is a better alternative to the loud backlash. I am here to say it is not: Unbeneficial factors in your life are only dragging you down because you let them be.

You must choose to fight the disease rather than the symptoms. I have learned that it is OK to cry after choosing to do the right thing. The regret and sorrow will only last for so long. You will then find yourself much happier as an individual. I have experienced this personally with relationships, sports, and other events and choices I make in life. I find myself mentally strong, happy, and positively outgoing because I choose to take control of my own life and my own choices. Fear not the consequences if you choose to act, think of the consequences if you choose to say or do nothing.

Poem:

Dumbbells.

There is no better therapist than the dumbbells on the rack.

When you pick them up, they feel everything you feel.

When you lift them, they will listen to everything you say

When you bench them, they will push you to be your best.

When you get calloused on your hands from using them so much, the dumbells are telling you, good job.

When you drop the dumbbells, you know it is you, not the dumbbell.

When you look at the dumbbells, they are challenging you to get stronger.

When you look at your arms in the mirror, admiring your own muscles in your arms, thank your dumbbells.

Dumbbells will never give you bad advice.

Dumbbells are worth more than that therapist you pay hundreds of dollars for.

Joey L.

As an older teen, I feel as though I have some knowledge to give to the young teens or even pre-teens. The advice I wish to share is to understand both sides of something. When I say this I intend for it to mean you can agree with your side of an argument, but teens must as well be open to new ideas or new knowledge to take in. Let's say you are in an argument with your parents about how to eat toast and you believe it should be eaten only with butter, however your parents say it is incredible with peanut butter. Without the belief in taking in new knowledge, you may never try this – but let's say you do try it and your mind has expanded into trying more things on toast. Most likely this philosophy will be used in more serious moments throughout a teen's life. Without this philosophy you essentially cannot grow as a human mentally because you are being weighed down by your own thoughts.

Jonathan S.

Among the many pieces of advice teenagers have been given throughout the course of their lives, I believe that the most important one of all is that teenagers must form their own opinions. These days, many sources of information have a chance of being biased and containing misinformation. This can extend to the people around you as well. This is why it is imperative for you to think for yourself. Believing everything you read or hear can cause you to make poor decisions that may worsen a situation. You must question anything you read from a news source, or hear from another person. You can't confirm something is true if you don't question it first. Questioning things can make your statements stronger when you're trying to explain your opinions to others. Next, you need to put in the effort to do some of your own research, and get all of the correct information. Acting as if you know what's going on when you really don't is a horrible trait to have. From your questions and research, form your own opinion on the issue, now that you have the most objective information possible. By doing your own research, and questioning what you read or hear, you strengthen your mind and opinions to make rational decisions.

Jonathan A.

The situation in our world right now that has stopped most of our lives is Covid-19. This is a really serious problem and it is slowing down the education system; finding jobs has been difficult and we have lost members of our lives due to this virus. December 12, 2019 is when this event started and it is currently January 2022! 2020 was the worst year that we have ever experienced and 2021 was slowly starting to get together. Events were brought out and schools reopened! 2022 is going to be the year that everything slowly starts to put itself together. No more needing a mask to go to your favorite store. No more worrying about your family getting harmed by an infection. No more social distancing. Everything will be okay. Wait: Everything is going to be GREAT!

Joshua N.

The ability to know yourself and others is one of the most important things to have right now in life. If you know yourself, you know where you want life to take you. To know yourself gives you confidence in who you are and gives you no hesitation in whatever path you choose in life. You cannot always have a rock to stand on when waters get high, so you must be your rock and be there for others when waters in their life get rough. Knowing yourself is to be collected and not in pieces. When rough waters come, and you are in pieces, you will scatter and be dragged to sea lost in the water, but if you are collected and secure, you will not wash away.

Joshua S.

When people get uncomfortable, they are pushed to do things differently. This is important and helpful as a teen because it forces you to make decisions that you typically wouldn't make. An article on CNBC.com says, "Many people are so comfortable they're miserable." This message explains that as you grow, you will grow out of certain things, people, and activities that you typically would enjoy earlier in your lifetime. As teens grow out of these things, they either stay comfortable in those places or they proceed to get uncomfortable and find new people and things to do. I know when you get uncomfortable, it helps you make smarter decisions and makes it easier to get out of peer pressure.

Josie

What I would say to someone struggling: No one's life is perfect, so when life is hard, count your blessings. You have shelter, safety, an opportunity to be educated and people who love you. Someone is dreaming of the life that you are living, so be thankful for everything you have. When you stop thinking so much about what you don't have, and start having gratitude for what you do have, you will find greater joy. Always look for the good and you will be amazed how much you find. Smell a flower, laugh at a joke, dance while you clean the kitchen, or take a deep breath of air. Life is so beautiful and is meant to be enjoyed.

Serve others. Stop thinking so much about yourself, and reach out to those who are struggling more than you. Somebody had a bad day today, and you smiling at them at the grocery store could help them feel hope. Talk to a friend, rake your neighbor's leaves, mail your friend a letter, or say thank you to a teacher. Your small act of love can change someone's day. Never underestimate the power of kindness and the effect it has on those around you.

Juan

One piece of advice I can give to any teen who is struggling at any point of their life is that all problems are but temporary. Doing something that you won't be able to take back is not worth the trouble – for example, suicide or committing violent acts toward younger siblings and friends. And if there's ever a day when you just can't take whatever you're going through, there are hotline numbers you can call at any time of day to just get whatever you're feeling off your chest. You don't have to go through whatever you're going through alone. There are people who care for you and people who can offer help and advice who have found themselves in the same situation.

Julianna

I wouldn't say I'm the most stereotypical teenager. But I also wouldn't say I'm unique in the ways that my brain works. There are many other teenagers, older and younger than me, that think similarly to the way that I do. I know the world isn't that great. I know we're still just teenagers, and through the eyes of the rest of the world, we're naive. And that's true. We are. But they are too. We know ourselves better than anyone else, even if that isn't that well. Right now, we should try to figure out who we are. Let's discover ourselves first, and then we'll have the chance to show people who we are. Everyone sees us as kids, children, someone they need to watch over. We might kind of be, sometimes. But we also know more about the world – OUR world – than many people will ever acknowledge. Do me, just an average girl, a favor, and be willing to discover and to be yourself. For me, it's the best decision I ever made.

Karlie

Everyone at some point has had the urge to fit in and has felt like they stand out from everyone else around them. Teens feel the need to fit in on social media, and in person. If you are feeling like no one likes you, your clothes aren't what everyone else is wearing, etc, you should take some time to figure out why you feel this way. Ask yourself if you even like what is trending at the moment. Is anyone actually judging you, or are they too focused on themselves? The attitude you have toward yourself is important. Find things you like about yourself to focus on, rather than focusing on the things you don't like about yourself. Be who you are and focus on the good.

Katelin

Covid-19 was a hard time for everyone. It was stressful, hard, and just terrible. One thing that has kept me going through these hard times is to remember that there is always a tomorrow. Every single day is different. Things change constantly. Getting stuck on one thing throughout the day is going to drag you down. Remember to think of the tomorrow, the better times, and the times without Covid-19. There will always be a tomorrow.

Kaya

Being a teenager is probably the hardest stage to get through in life. Everything feels like a challenge, wanting to do good but not having the motivation, or even just all of a sudden hating yourself. So hard on ourselves for what? You are doing the best you can and I'm proud of you for that so keep going. It's hard to write advice for someone you don't know because you can't take into account all that they have been through. One piece of advice might be translated differently through other people, but if I had to pick one piece of advice that I wish I would have followed as a young teenager, it would be to just experience life before it's too late. I don't mean give up on school and stop caring about everything, what I mean is to start viewing everything as an opportunity rather than a challenge. Go out and experience things that you might find difficult, talk to people you don't know, ask questions about everything. Experience these things now because soon you won't have the time to. Open your eyes to different opinions and cultures, start discovering who you are and who you really want to be. As adulthood approaches all of us, these experiences will become extremely helpful in the future. Don't let other people distract you from what you want, and don't make time for the people who have tried to stop you. They feed off attention because it makes them look "cool." So, after taking the time to read this, I hope you gained some valuable insight on how to overcome your teenage years. I promise it will get better, no matter how awful it seems right now.

Keegan

As the sun falls ending the day

The mind runs wild in its dream world

The darkness surrounds it

It doesn't stop running, it chases the light

Logan

The advice that is most vital in high school is to make good friends, not more friends.

Something that you will eventually learn and experience is the people you are hanging out with today will not be the people you are eating lunch with in 3 years. "Friends" will come into your life like change at a register, in your pocket and then lost without thought. If you can find good friends who have similar interests – whether it be work, fun, or play – you can then create goals and help each other achieve them as a team, which is a powerful tool. Having a solid group of friends helping each other and feeding off each other can create infinite opportunities and possibilities. You really can achieve anything. Friends might not last, but good friends do, and you should take advantage of being young and having this opportunity because most people take it for granted. Don't worry so much about being cool or being a football star or being what you think others like. After high school, people forget, and the real world comes into effect. Be ahead of the game, have goals, surround yourself with people who want to win, not just want to be in high school.

Lucas

During the Covid-19 pandemic, you can expect to face many kinds of challenges – making friendships, keeping friendships, losing friendships, family problems, educational engagement, and physical activity motivation. Your best opportunity to keep away from these things is to think. You don't need to make irrational decisions based on what you think is right or what you think is best for you at that time. If you're able to think about what might happen and how it will affect others, you will be able to overcome most of the challenges you might face during the Covid-19 pandemic by taking care of yourself and making new friendships.

Mabel

Some of the happiest-seeming people are really the saddest. You never know what people are dealing with and how they feel on the inside. Be kind to everyone, do things for others, and make sure your friends are okay because if you don't, you might not get to talk to them again. More people are depressed than ever before so stay safe and do your best to cheer people up.

Madison

Mental health

We tend to forget the importance

Do you find yourself feeling numb

Having no hope or motivation

Feeling lost and like you have no place here

Thinking you have no purpose

Remember your self worth

You belong here

You are worth it

You are loved more than you know

You can hold the world in your hands

Remember your self worth

Maddy B.

Remember when you were 5? Running around the yard with your siblings or friends, watching raindrops race down the car window, playing tag or hide and seek. Back then it seemed like we would never grow up, or ever be a "big kid." But now being an adult is just a couple blinks away, and the realization of moving away from the one thing you have ever truly known is starting to set in. The feeling of growing up becomes so catastrophic because there is no way to escape. Yet again, though, as teenagers, don't we like the thrill of challenging the old and becoming new? Even though we have no idea what we are doing, we can do it, because there are more opportunities in the future than we can even imagine!

Madaline

In 2020, we teens experienced something that we can all agree truly changed our lives. The Covid-19 pandemic hit us by surprise and we got taken out of school without any idea when we'd be back to see our friends and teachers again. Those months were very scary. What I wish somebody could've told me then is that things will look up from here. It felt like I hit rock bottom and I wish somebody could've told me that things will go back to normal eventually. If I had known that, I wouldn't have spent those months stressed, overwhelmed, and feeling alone. During scary times we should stay positive even when it seems very difficult to do.

Marco

During the COVID-19 pandemic, emotional and physical hardships can occur. Finding hobbies are a great way to traverse through the pandemic. These hobbies could include cooking, playing video games, playing a sport, or reading. Staying fit is also a necessity whilst being out of school and sports for a long while. Walking and biking are simple ways to stay fit, while lifting weights and running are more intense options. Personally, I kept my mind and body occupied by lifting weights and playing basketball over the long pandemic. Emotional problems can occur at any time, so having someone you can trust and talk to is always recommended.

Mariah

Dear anyone who needs to hear this: Growing up in the world today, during these hard times, comes with many challenges and temptations. Covid affected EVERYONE in different ways. Straight A students started to fail. Some lost jobs, people they loved and even hope. High school is hard for everyone and the pandemic didn't make it any easier.

The people around you will love to tell you all the ways you are broken and can be "fixed" to be able to fit societal expectations. Don't ever rely on anyone's acceptance but your own. Learn to be independent and try not to lose who you are by trying to fit in with other people. Everyone is fighting their own personal battles, but when it comes to school we are thinking similar thoughts. Things can get hard and you will lose people along the way, but the ones who were willing to stay are the only ones good enough to keep anyways. Try to say "hi" to new people even if they are considered "weird," because, who knows, they could become your next best friend, or maybe your simple "hi" made their day. Learn to be there for yourself, and pay attention to your own needs and mental health. Mental health is more important than your grades! If you are struggling to find hope in life, then you need to find it before you need to stress about school. Staying alive and happy is more important than a letter grade. Know that people change and friends will come and go, so stay strong in yourself. Don't let anyone take you for granted, you don't need to be with someone if it hurts more to be with them then without. Toxic relationships hurt both people involved, leave them for the good of both of you. Don't take anything you have for granted, life can change in the blink of an eye. Be grateful for what you have, nothing is forever. Find who you are as a person and make your own opinions but never be rude to those with different views as you. Know that talking bad about someone shows more of who you are as a person than who you're talking about. Lastly, try to help the next generation of teens to come and make the world a better and more accepting place. We all have had our ups and downs during these hard times, but through it all we should continue to get back up again.

Mario

If I had to give any kind of advice to teenagers now and in the near future, It would be to keep an open mind. Many people these days are manipulative and are bad influences that will push their beliefs onto you or pressure you to do what they say or think, so keep an eye on who you hang out with. I have two half-sisters, and since I was young, their family on their dad's side has tried to change the way my sisters think by pressuring or insulting them and would lie to gain their trust. I am not saying not to trust others; however, you should always be careful in whom you place trust and keep an eye out for people who do bad things. With that being said, stay positive and good luck.

Matthew

Lies require commitment. Lying can get you in really big trouble. Take it from me, I've been a liar all my life. Lying is really easy to make a habit but really hard to break. A big reason I lie is out of fear, and that might be the reason you lie too. Lying will in the end get you in even more trouble. Small or big things you lie about will get you into problems and lose trust from the people you love. A way to overcome it is to remind yourself you could lose something very important to you if you lie. Another way to overcome this big obstacle is just to have a positive mindset about it all.

Meagan

The advice that I can give to teens is to take it easy and slow. Don't let school push you past your boundaries; do what you can do, even if it's the bare minimum. Your health is much more of a priority than your grades or homework. I've stood exactly where you have, I've felt the exhaustion first hand. It's tiring having the weight on your shoulders, isn't it? So take a break. Put down the pencil, close the computer and go do something that brings you joy. Go outside, take a walk, eat your favorite foods, enjoy life, appreciate it, and do what you can.

Mia

Overcoming the obstacles of Covid-19 are huge. Covid-19 has affected everyone in their own way. Some tips and tricks to keep the days from passing by like a calendar could be sleeping more often and trying out new hobbies at home. One thing that helped me a lot through this time that's not super common but is super fun is learning how to sew. My mother has taught me how to use the sewing machine and how to stitch old used shirts or clothing that has holes. Another thing I enjoyed learning was knitting. Knitting stuffed animals and such with my grandmother has taught me so much about her and kept me busy. I know I sound like a grandmother, but these hobbies are actually very fun and were a good way to keep my mind straight.

Keira

Many people say that being a teenager is the best part of your life. Or is it? Older generations, like baby boomers, seem to have this mindset. We have significantly grown from other generations; we see more technology, more mental illness, more people going undiagnosed, and unfortunately, during the Covid-19 pandemic, a spike in domestic abuse. Your teenage years are a critical part of your life; it is what shapes you as a person. But not everybody's teenage years are similar or even the best. Most teenagers like you and I struggle with body-image issues, social comparison insecurities, anxiety, and depression, but this doesn't diminish your life's importance. Comparing yourself to others will only bring you down. Even when it's a struggle to break this habit, you must try. You're your own unique person with attributes that nobody else has. You shouldn't disregard your trauma; you must build upon it and not let it hold you back. You know what you've gone through, and that is what's important. Some people say that their teenage years were the best part of their life, but why only constrict it to a few years. Make your entire life the best you can, even with hardships; it's what lets you grow as a person.

Natalie

This day and age it's hard to not compare yourself to others, whether it's on social media or real life. If you're constantly worried about what others think and do, you won't make it very far in life – you'll constantly be creating roadblocks that will be impossible to overcome. Comparing yourself to others can cause many problems in your life: It can lead to depression, self doubt, and anxiety, and can ultimately damage your self image. This just sets you up for failure later in life when it's time to make those big decisions. You will be too focused on what others would do in the situation, which will cause you to get lost in your own thoughts and lose your true self. In the end, the only person you should compare yourself to is the person you were yesterday and who you want to become.

Nick

The most valuable piece of advice you could incorporate into your own life is to formulate your own opinion on things and think for yourself. This will aid you in discovering your true desires as well as what your moral compass supports, and can also encourage some to branch out and discover new avenues in life. Forming opinions also helps develop social skills which include debating, disagreeing and critical thinking, all things that will put you in a better position when transitioning into adulthood. Through the many negatives that came with the Covid-19 pandemic, it has also been a massive learning experience for those around the world. A wake-up call, some might say. The first-hand exposure to these worldwide events has made a whole generation of people stronger for the years ahead of them.

Noah

This pandemic has done a lot of damage to the mental state of teens like us. In the beginning, it wasn't that bad: Wear a mask, it'll be over soon. Almost 22 months later, it's still not over, and there's a new variant now. Most of our mental states aren't too good anymore. Some want to cry, others are just angry, and some just want to lay down and sleep out the pandemic. But we shouldn't keep in tears or anger. As fantastic a feeling it is to try to sleep out the pandemic, instead we should cry, let out the built-up anger and try to get out of bed. You need to try and change how you go about the pandemic. For example, take up a sport of some kind like boxing, martial arts, really almost anything that's available. Try and work out. Even if you can't go to gyms or have the money for all the expensive equipment, you can still go for walks, jog, or if you can, bike. I know myself I don't want to get out of bed and go for a run or even get out of bed, but you need to.

The change won't be instant. You won't wake up and immediately get out of bed and run two miles. You'll have to take it slow and find what you want to do. It doesn't have to be physical. You could stop eating as much junk food, or learn how to cook – but do something. It will help.

Nolan

A Message to Insecurity

When you glance in a mirror

Why does your reflection glare back at you in a state
of fear?

Why do you gawk at them? they aren't you

You are you

"Trust me" says the puppeteered mirror of fear

"this imperfection

Was never here."

Olivia A.

Every teen goes through obstacles, whether you see it or not. Many teenagers suffer from depression or anxiety and many more things. You may go through similar problems. You'll never know what is going on in every teen's life at home or outside of the house. Everyone has their way of getting through hard times. Ways to overcome an obstacle include having a good mindset, being positive, and knowing that everything will be okay in the end. Never give up! Keep going. Move forward even if you don't think you can, and surround yourself with friends and family who care about you. That will help you overcome your depression and continue to fight your depression and never give up. You can stay positive by looking up positive or inspirational quotes and limiting social media and other apps that will cause your mindset to be hostile. An essential piece of advice is to always ask for help. Asking for help isn't a bad thing; some will think so, but in the end, it's helping you fight for your life and allow yourself to be with your depression and anxiety. Let's be honest here: You need to have confidence in yourself and know you are stronger than you think you are. Allow yourself to be who you are and not what others want you to be. There will be challenges along the way but knowing you can overcome them positively is key to facing those challenges.

Olivia B.

I feel all teens should know that if you are going to bother arguing with someone, make sure to understand what they believe. Is there any point in arguing with someone who will not listen to anything you say or the other way around? Why should they have to listen to whatever you say if they feel what you believe is wrong? If neither side will take the time to listen to each other, then all you did was waste time and energy. Even if you feel that the other side is full of lies, you still should listen so you can figure out where a miscommunication could have happened. Knowing both sides give you an advantage since you will know the "whole picture" instead of the fraction of your side of the story. In the end, please take the time to understand the other side of the story as it makes you more knowledgeable and helps the argument not just be a waste of time.

Pedro

What I have to say about the pandemic and to teens is that this pandemic is a pandemic where people are depressed, sad, mad, etc. Why? Because the world isn't the same anymore. But I think even though this pandemic is bad, I feel as if you need to control yourself, you need to adapt to things that come to this world. You can't just lose yourself because things are bad right now. I feel like things happen for a reason. And when those things come, you need to not lose what you have or what you want to accomplish, you can't just give up.

Rebecca

The best piece of advice I can give you is to take care of yourself and always put yourself first, no matter what anyone says. Just because you put yourself first doesn't mean you are being selfish or inconsiderate; it means you are a strong individual who is taking control of your life during these hard times. Taking care of yourself should be mentally and physically, like meditating to clear your mind, or working out to work on your health. When you don't take care of yourself, your mental health can drop drastically, which is why self care has been such a popular subject during this pandemic.

At the end of the day all you have is yourself. Friends are going to come and go as well as other relationships, but you will always have yourself, so why not just take care of you for a change? Some people will make excuses like they don't have time but everyone has time for themselves. You could use the time that you find yourself scrolling on social media instead of doing something for your mind or body. That is the best advice I think all teens should hear right now.

Rebel

During your time as a teen, the most important advice that I can offer you is to take care of your body. We go through a lot of things as teens and our body goes through them with us. You only get one body for your whole life; you should cherish and love yourself and your body. I know that it is easier said than done but with the right people around you, it gets easier every day. Your body is still developing, and mentally and physically your body needs to be taken care of. As a junior in high school, I know that it is extremely hard to love yourself and have confidence with constantly seeing "perfect" bodies on social media or walking down the street. This can lead you to hold yourself to an invisible standard that no one else sees but you. With the right people around you, they should help you or encourage you to love yourself. If they aren't there for you, you need to learn how to look in the mirror and say that you are perfect in your own way and no one can change who you are. It takes time and I know that from personal experience, but it's never too late to start – now.

Reese

Don't care what others think about you. You shouldn't be worried about what others think of you because then you might feel obligated to change to fulfill their liking of you. If you keep changing just to make other people happy, eventually you might not be happy with yourself because you won't feel like the real you. You might feel like you're faking your way through life just to try to get people to like you. Soon enough you will find people who like you for who you really are.

Rhiley

I spent so many years trying to impress others and trying to be normal so I would not get judged. But what really is "normal" – is that even a thing? There are constantly people who might be judging you or not, but we always think that others are judging us no matter what. Say they are. Why do you even care so much about what they are thinking? Your life is not theirs. You are your own person who gets to choose what you want to do with your life and how you want to spend it.

We spend so much time thinking about what others care about us and it is mentaly draining, coming from experience. You need to stop caring so much about what others think of you because, let me tell you, once you stop caring about others' opinions about your life, it feels like you took so much weight off your shoulders. It feels like you can breathe again. All the things that you think that people are judging you for, they probably are not. The biggest person to judge you is yourself. You just need to stop thinking about it so much and just go on with your life. Once you do you will feel much better.

Ronaldo

Life is hard but you have got to keep on fighting and always believe in yourself to achieve your goals and dreams. You just must go through those tough times to find yourself and what you're capable of. But to get through it you must set a goal for yourself and surround yourself with people who will help you, But, it's on you to take the first step toward a greater journey. Everyone goes through these times – just remember to keep your head up and keep fighting. One of my goals is to graduate from college and find a job that I will love and be happy and enjoy life because it goes by fast.

Rose

Overcoming an obstacle can be difficult but you must remember that this too shall pass. The more you look at the problem, the more it starts to consume. All your thoughts are only about this obstacle. It starts to make you feel numb inside with anxiety. Don't let those things control your life. Always push for overcoming the barrier, not being pessimistic toward it. As a teenager, every wall you climb, either good or bad, will teach you a lesson you can hold onto for life. Don't let the nasty obstacles define you. Remember, there is always a tomorrow, a future. As a teen, some obstacles you may face are finding your identity, who you want to be, and how you want others to see you. Other barriers can include a first job, first car, first payment, etc. Your attitude towards obstacles should be determination. Finally, you need to be the one who overcomes obstacles. You cannot play the victim; you must realize that the situation is good or bad. You cannot blame others for it to feel sympathy. You will feel confident and assertive if you handle your problem and not pass it on to others. Like

Gwendolyn Brooks says, "Even if you are not ready for the day, it cannot always be night." Everybody should live by that because nobody should be in the dark about their obstacles. Remember, you got this! Do not let an obstacle, great or small, determine who you are.

Saphryn

damaged youth.

i know you feel alone,

and that your house is not a home,

these years have made it hard to grow,

but I know that you can do it

you question each one of your friends;

are they true, or just pretending?

as if you wait upon the ending,

for the moment they choose to leave

i am right there with you,

you're not alone, you aren't a fool,

these troubled times created damaged youth,

but we will make it through, somehow

just stand your ground,

look at all of those around you,

and know that you are loved,

even when your scars are shining through

you are worth more than what these years have made
of you,

you are more than just a piece of this damaged youth,

your voice matters,

your feelings matter,

your struggles matter

you.

you matter.

and don't you ever forget it.

Sergio

It's been almost two years and we still don't seem to get out of this pandemic. That's OK though, because I know you'll make it through, my heart and soul tell me so. Allow me to tell you something: The simple fact that you are here, reading this, tells me you are strong. It tells me you have the willpower inside of you to face the rest of this pandemic and further challenges ahead that lay along your path of life. Do not allow yourself to be chained down by anything or anyone, I know how it feels to be chained down and feel defeated; you are stronger than that. I won't say it'll be a walk in the park but you are capable of exceeding the expectations you may have for yourself by miles.

All in all, you, a teenager, have a lot to give, my friend. Second, you have the power within you to become something great, but you cannot allow yourself to be beaten down by all the bad. You have the soul of a raging Phoenix. I wish I could have met you to tell you this in person but all regrets aside, stay strong, stay healthy, remember to eat, play, and hold those you care deeply for close to your heart. Godspeed, my friend.

Steve

There are people in the world who are having problems at a young age For example, some teens have had to overcome the struggle of not having a parent figure in their life that would show them right from wrong. They have to accept that their parent figure, or birth parents, won't be coming back to them and accept that life can be cruel at times but can be good at times.

Teens also are faced with the fact that some people won't listen to them because they are too young or they wouldn't understand what's going on. Teens need to show that they have a voice and that just because they are young, they can understand what is going on and give their opinion about what to do. They are also faced with expectations to know everything that they are told. But even though they are taught what they need to learn, it takes time for certain teens to process what they learned and remember what they were taught. They need to ask for help or tell the teacher to take it slow so that they can learn without being overwhelmed.

Taylor

You need to be the bigger person. It's time to grow up. Being a teenager means you're at a turning point in your life. Your actions now may help to determine the path of the rest of your life. It is extremely important to be able to handle arguments or disagreements in your life correctly. This is why the best advice I could possibly give you or any teen is to try and understand both sides of everything. When that girl disrespects you or that guy hits your car and you are going to punch them in the face, stop. Have a conversation about it; handle it in a different way. That girl is insecure about herself because her mom said mean things to her all her life and now she says mean things to others. That guy hit your car because his grandma just died and he couldn't think clearly. There are always two sides to everything and it is so very important to consider both sides before deciding how to handle a situation. Acting out in situations like these will only lead to destroyed relationships, feelings of resentment and even criminal charges. You have reached the time in your life when your decisions really have an impact. Save that relationship, don't ruin your life by ending up in jail. All it takes is a little bit of mutual understanding.

Teegan

Whether it's at school, or at home, work hard. Having a good work ethic is one of the most important things to have. Sometimes it may be hard to keep going, but I guarantee you, the reward is well worth it. Well worth the time, energy, blood, sweat. School was never really my thing so I made up for it in the weight room, pushing myself everyday, at work, making sure I was the first one there and the last one to leave. You might be tired, angry, depressed. Use that to your advantage and give everything your all.

Thomas

The worst type of stress that you will encounter at school is insecurity. Before the pandemic, I was in a very different mindset. In 9th grade I had ´friends" that didnt treat me right, and I was basically included so they could laugh at me and make me do stupid stuff. When you're already insecure about yourself, and people are using you just to laugh at you, it basically destroys your confidence. And it wasn't just a few people, it was six all together. Also, I had a lot of religious friends whom I learned later were not very accepting of me. During the quarantine, I had so much time to myself that I started to realize just how bad I was treated. Looking back, it's kind of shocking seeing how differently I would react now to what they were saying. I'd sometimes question if I was just sensitive, but I remembered having dozens of conversations with them about looks and personal stuff in general. They knew I was struggling with confidence, but the toxicity continued. Now coming back to school, I know how to respond and avoid situations where I may feel uncomfortable. I'm not saying that quarantine was a good thing (because it certainly was not), but being with my family for over a year was really good for me. This was especially true because my sister and her husband stayed with us along with their dog Ellie, while they sold their house, and we watched horror movies every night. So my advice would be to find good people that are fun to be around, and to push away anyone that is causing more harm than good.

Travis

My advice for you would be to stop spending so much energy on what others think of you. I understand that you can't just stop worrying about what they think of you, but don't let it stress you out. At the end of the day it doesn't matter if that random person that you barely know thinks you look good or bad. The only person that you need to impress is yourself. Everyone will have an opinion of you, and if you try to please everyone you will drive yourself crazy.

Trent

As a kid that went through the pandemic and is still going through the pandemic, I understand that there will be tough times. There will be times where you think that the world is over and that you won't make it out. I have had those days. Recently my sister and I were at my grandparents' house and she got in a pretty big accident. She rolled a four wheeler going pretty fast and flew into a railroad tie, knocked that over and hit a fence and rolled that as well. I was the first responder to the situation and I was the only person for around a quarter mile around her. I still have bad days thinking about that and there were often times I didn't think she would recover. She had a broken wrist and she had a huge concussion. She doesn't remember that day and I always say I'm fine. But the memory of riding up to her, her laying in the grass with the four wheeler tipped over and still running, all the blood around the area and my sister laying unconscious still burns in my mind. This isn't about me, though. This is for the kids that think that it doesn't get any better. Trust me, it does. It may not be instant but I promise you that it will. It'll take some time and it'll take some healing but you will make it out of the hole and you will be better than before. It may not seem like much advice, but it definitely helps to know that there are people around that would rather be at your side than at your grave. You are loved beyond what you could imagine by many and there are so many things that you are missing out on in life if you leave. Life will go on and it will get better, trust me. Crying isn't a bad thing and it actually helps remove bad toxins in your system, so if you ever need to, go ahead and cry. You won't be made fun of, you won't be called names because of it, you'll help the healing process and you will be a better person because of it.

Trevor N.

We all have had at least one thing that we struggle with. For some of you it might be struggling with how you look, or how you dress. For others it might be eating, or an addiction. This world is more broken than you think, and it is too far gone to be fixed to any extent that could matter, but I believe that we can do enough to keep it together. The only thing we can do is surround ourselves with the people who want to see us succeed, because they are the ones who will stick with us until the end of the line. If there is a struggle with purpose in your life, all you must remember is that there are always people who are rooting for you. The only thing you need to do is reach out and ask that question. Life is too short to live a life where you look back to what you could have done. To live is to breathe, to breathe is to be alive, and to be alive is to love and be loved, to be loved is to know the true and real love of God.

Zakary

Your life will have some ups and downs – everyone has those – but you need both to have a good life. During these past few years, many people have felt that life isn't going their way right now, due to many different things, but mainly the pandemic. Many people's lives revolve around being around others and spending time with them, but most, if not all relationships have been put on hold, which is hard for many people. So people have been wondering if this nightmare will ever get better, and my answer is yes. It always does.

Many people don't realize, but your life is constantly going up. Sometimes you'll have something terrible happen, and it will seem like your life is falling apart, but that's not always true because after all the dust settles, your life will start going up again, and it always will. So if you feel like your life isn't going to be great right now, just remember that after all the bad things are over, your life will always get better. The most important thing to remember is, you need to have some bad days to appreciate the good ones.

CPSIA information can be obtained
at www.ICGtesting.com
Printed in the USA
BVHW070221110522
636630BV00011B/1137

9 781977 250698